# SADIE

# MEETS  A

# MONARCH

Written by Nancy Zimmerman and

Illustrated by Rebekah Raffield

Book 4 in Sadie's Great Adventures

## HEDGEHOG HILL PRESS

An imprint of NJZ Enterprises

NJZ Enterprise
PO Box 3148
Anderson, IN 46018

Nzbestself.com

A Hedgehog Hill Press original, 2017

**ISBN:  978-0692560051**

## DEDICATION

This is dedicated to Loretta Heiniger who has shared her love of butterflies with hundreds of people throughout the years. She has saved them, raised them, and shared that love freely.

# SADIE

# MEETS A

# MONARCH

"Hurry, hurry!" Cheyenne urged Sadie.

"I am getting ready as fast as I can," Sadie laughed as she combed her hair.

Amelia, Naomi, Cheyenne, and Sadie were going to walk down to Loretta's. Loretta was a friend of Cheyenne's Nana and she raised butterflies. The girls were very excited to go see her. She had many kinds of butterfly eggs that she would hatch and release but they were mostly interested in the Monarch.

Sadie had never seen a Monarch except in pictures. Scotland didn't have any Monarchs.

After the girls were given last minute instructions by Emma, Sadie's mother, they headed out.

As they went through the playground, Gideon and Jay were there. "Hey, where are you going?" Gideon asked.

"We are going to Loretta's." Naomi replied.

"Can we come too?" Jay asked

"Darn!" Cheyenne exclaimed. "You will have to go ask your moms and that will take more time. No, you can't."

"Hey, Cheyenne, it won't take that much more time really." said Amy.

"Oh, I guess you are right," Cheyenne replied. "So, go ask your moms……… and hurry!

Naomi and Amy grinned at each other Cheyenne was always in a hurry and sometimes she got pretty bossy.

The boys returned after getting permission to go with them.

"Let's go thru the butterfly garden so we can tell Loretta the butterflies that are there today!" suggested Naomi.

"Race ya there," Gideon said to his friend Jay and the two boys began running ahead to the butterfly garden.

Amelia turned to Sadie. "Have you had a chance to visit the garden since you have been here?" she asked.

"No, I haven't," said Sadie as they got to the garden and began on the pathway that curved around some big

rocks. "Ooh. It is beautiful." she exclaimed as the kids continued through the garden to Loretta's.

Cheyenne stepped up to the door and knocked while they all waited.

"Hello there," Loretta said kindly as she opened the door to her butterfly nursery. She had a screened in back porch where she kept her "babies." That was what she called all of the different stages of the butterflies.

"Hi, Loretta," said Naomi. "This is our new friend, Sadie. She is here from Scotland for a while and she has never seen a real live Monarch."

"Well, Sadie, I think you are in for a treat," Loretta said with a smile. She invited the kids over to have some cookies and lemonade. Gideon, Jay, and Sadie had not been to Loretta's before so they were excited to see what

they were going to learn today.

All of the kids loved the butterfly garden at the apartments and spent hours in the summer enjoying both the flowers and the butterflies that were there. Loretta had helped some of the girls' mothers to plan and plant the garden for everyone to enjoy. One year the newspaper even came and took pictures of it and some of the kids had their picture taken.

When they were done with the treats, Loretta led the kids over to her bins where the butterflies were in different stages. Loretta began talking about the life cycle of the butterfly and the kids listened carefully.

"When we talk about butterflies, the way they change is called *metamorphosis*." she began.  They have four stages of development.  They will go from an egg to a caterpillar to a chrysalis and finally emerge into a butterfly.

Do you have any questions?

"Yes," said Naomi.  "Where do they lay their eggs?"

"Well, that is a very good question, Naomi." Loretta said with a smile.

"A butterfly will lay an egg on a special plant that it chooses.  The plant will be food for the caterpillar when it hatches from the egg.  Every kind of butterfly has a different kind of plant that the caterpillar or larva eat.

# BUTTERFLY EGGS:

MONARCH

QUESTION MARK

CABBAGE WHITE

RED ADMIRAL

SILVER SPOTTED SKIPPER

WILD INDIGO DUSKYWING

BLACK SWALLOW

TAIL

HACKBERRY EMPORER

SPICEBUSH

SWALLOW-TAIL

TIGER

SWALLOW-TAIL

WEST VIRGINIA

WHITE

YELLOW SULPHUR

"How does it know what plant is right?" asked Jay.

"That is what nature does for our animals," replied Loretta. "It gives the animals all the information they need to take care of themselves. If you do not have the kind of plant a butterfly needs to lay its egg in your garden, it will go to different gardens until it finds a plant that will do. This is why it is important to know what kinds of butterflies are in the area so that you can plant the kind of plants they can lay eggs on."

"Is that why there are so many kinds of plants in our butterfly garden at the apartments?" Cheyenne asked.

MONARCHS ♡'s MILKWEED!

SPICEBUSH SWALLOWTAIL ♡'s SPICEBUSH!

PAINTED LADIES ♡ THISTLES!

TIGER SWALLOWTAIL ♡'s WILLOW FLOWERS!

RED ADMIRAL ♡'s WILD CHERRY FLOWERS

SILVER SPOTTED SKIPPER ♡'s WISTERIA

"Yes. We all know the kinds of butterflies there are in the area so we just made sure we had the plants the adult butterflies needed to lay their eggs on. I think we did a very good job, don't you?"

"Oh, yes," said Amy. "It is beautiful to look at and there are so many different kinds of butterflies there. You did a very good job."

"Are there any other questions now" Loretta asked before she want on to the next stage of development. "Let's look and see if any of the eggs have hatched overnight. If they have, we need to move them to a different bin." While she opened the bins and took each

plant and looked at the underside of the leaves where the eggs were she told them, "Different kinds of butterflies lay different kinds of eggs.  These are plants that Monarchs lay their eggs on."  There were many plants and some had hatched out tiny little caterpillars.  She handed each of the children a plant with a caterpillar for them to hold.  Some of the caterpillars had crawled to the side and were eating the leaves of the plant.

"Let's open this first bin.  Hand me your plants and we will put these little "babies" in here so they can go ahead and eat."  Each of the plants in the bin had a caterpillar on it, some had two or three.  "They travel around and eat on different plants when they are here.

That is why we need to have screens on the bin."

"So they won't get out and crawl around your house?" piped up Jay.

"Exactly," she laughed.  "I love my babies, but I don't want them where I might step on them."

"Or eat them if they get in your cereal," Cheyenne and everyone joined in at the idea.

"No," laughed Loretta, "I certainly wouldn't want that. Now that you have seen these little ones, let's look at how quickly they grow"  They stepped over to the next two bins where the caterpillars were larger. Then in the next bin they were bigger yet.  At the last bin, Loretta took one of the plants out and took it back over to the first bin to compare to the first ones.

"Wow!" said Amelia. "That is amazing. They are so much bigger than they are at first."

"Yes, as they grow they shed their skin five times. Every time they shed their skin, it is called an *instar*. After the fifth time, they form a chrysalis." She put the larger caterpillar back in the bin and they went to the final two bins where there were caterpillars attaching themselves to the top screen.

"Why are they hanging there?" asked Jay.

"That is what they do when they are ready to form the chrysalis. Oh, look," she pointed to one of the bins.

The kids looked as the caterpillar split open and began to fold the skin around itself and within just a very short time the chrysalis had been formed. It was a

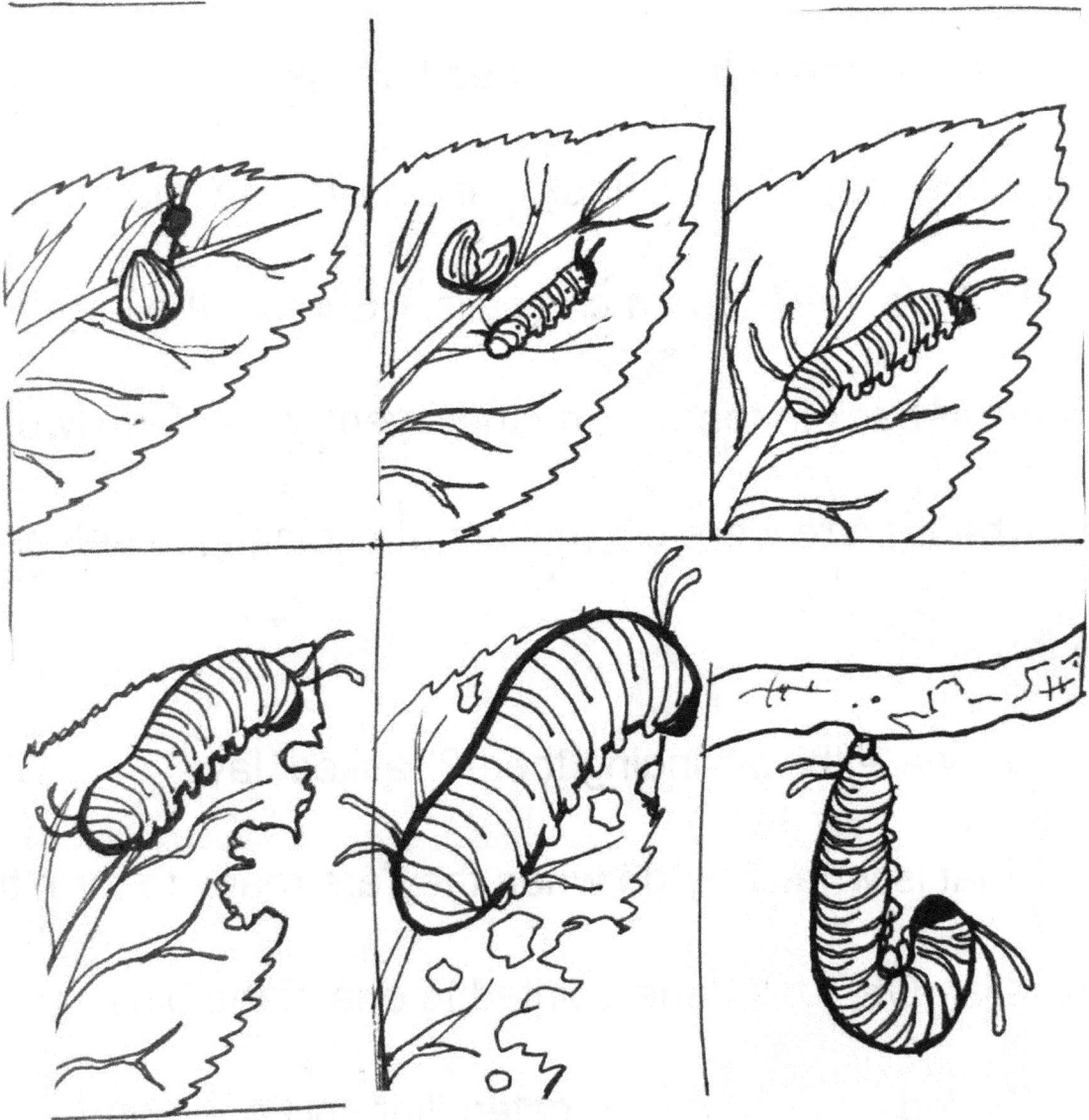

beautiful pale green and looked like it had dots made of gold around the top.

"Ooh," the kids began talking among themselves about what they had seen. The boys went back to the second bin and began comparing the sizes of the caterpillars. Naomi and Cheyenne watched to see if any more of the caterpillars would turn into a chrysalis.

Loretta let them look as long as they wanted to because she knew how interesting it could be.

Amelia, looked very thoughtful then asked Loretta, "What happens when they are in the chrysalis to get them to become a butterfly?"

"You are all asking really good questions," Loretta told

her, "but let's wait just a minute until everyone is finished

then I will tell you about what happens next.

The kids began coming back over to where Loretta

and Amy were talking.  "Now I am going to show you the

very last bin," she said.

They all walked to the next table where there were

many chrysalides. (Loretta explained that this word means

more than one chrysalis and is called a plural word.)

"Oh, my gosh!  There  are HUNDREDS!" Cheyenne

exclaimed.  "Look, some of them have already hatched"

"Yes, that is what I want you to see.  Once they hatch,

they need to be left alone until their wings dry or they will

not be able to fly.  Once they are all hatched in

each bin, we release them into a garden." said Loretta as she moved toward a bin sitting over on a different table.

"This bin has eighteen Monarchs that hatched out during the day yesterday and this morning. I think twelve of them are ready to be released. Would you all like to help me do that?"

The kids all began talking at the same time while smiling, laughing, and some of them were even clapping their hands they were so excited.

Loretta took the bin outside and sat it in the sun on the picnic table. She had them line up with Sadie being first. She reached in and got one of the butterflies. "Now, if you will look carefully, you will see the difference between the boy butterflies and the girl butterflies. The boys have a

black dot on their lower wings.  See?"  She gave each of

the children time to see the black dot then she turned to

Sadie.  "Are  you ready to release the first one?"

"Yes," Sadie giggled.  "I think I am.  What do I need to

do?"

"You just hold your hand out and I will put the butterfly

on the palm of your hand."  Loretta showed them by

putting it on her hand.  The butterfly stayed there for a

minute and walked over to the side of Loretta's hand and

she turned it so the butterfly was walking on the outside of

it.  The butterfly stayed there briefly before it flew off.

"Now, if you are ready, Sadie, I will get one out for you to

release."

Sadie was excited to have a butterfly on her hand and

did as Loretta had instructed.  While they were watching it

crawl around on Sadie's hand, they looked to see if it had the black dots on its bottom wing. It did, so they knew it was a boy also.

When Naomi took her turn, the butterfly Loretta put on her palm did not have the dots of a male, so they all knew it was a girl. So it went until they had all had two turns releasing butterflies. There was one left so it was decided that Sadie should get to release that since she was the newest member of the group.

When the children left, they remembered to thank Loretta for their refreshments and for the chance to release some butterflies with her. She smiled and invited them back as they turned to leave and go home.

Sadie went back and hugged Loretta and gave her a special kiss on the cheek as a thank you for such a lovely time.  She then ran after the others as she waved goodbye.

## Butterfly fun facts

- Butterflies taste with their feet.

- Butterflies do not have mouths.

- Butterflies need sun to fly.

- Butterflies fly during the day.

- Butterflies can see some colors. They can see red, yellow, and green.

- Butterflies cannot fly if they are too cold.

- They need to be warm to fly.

- Butterflies have 4 wings

- There are about 20,000 different kinds of butterflies in the world

- The wings of a butterfly are transparent. The wings of a butterfly have tiny scales. These give their wings color. This is why they do not look transparent to us.

# Bibliography

Many books are available in your local bookstore and on Amazon. This is a list to get you started.

- *Butterfly, Butterfly: A Book of Colors,* Petr Horacek for Ages 3-7 Grades K-3
- *Butterfly: Colors and Counting,* Jerry Pallotta, Preschool
- *Are You a Butterfly?* Judy Allen, ages 5-8, Grades K-3
- *10 Little Caterpillars.* Bill Martin Jr., Ages 2-8, Grades D-3
- *Waiting for Wings,* Lois Ehlert, Ages 4-7 Grades K-3
- *Where Butterflies Grow,* Joanne Ryder, Ages 5-8 Grades K-3
- *Explore My World, Butterflies,* Marie Ferguson Delamo Ages 3-7 Grades Preschool-2
- *National Geographic Readers: Caterpillar to Butterfly,* Laura Marsh Ages 4-6 Grades Preschool-1
- *Clara Caterpillar,* Pamela Duncan Edwards, Ages 3-6 Grades Preschool-1
- *Monarch Butterfly,* Gail Gibbons, Ages 5-8 Grades K-3
- *My, Oh My, a Butterfly,* Tish Rabe, Ages 4-8 Grades K-3
- *From Caterpillar to Butterfly,* Debrah Heiligman Ages 4-8 Grades K-3
- *Velma Gratch and the Way Cool Butterfly,* Alan Madison Ages 4-8 Grades K-3

# BUTTERFLY GARDENING BOOKS

There are many wonderful books on butterfly gardening and you may have local butterfly gardens you can visit.  Another resource would be the local Master Gardener's chapter or you County Extension Agent.

- *Super Simple Butterfly Gardens*  by Alex Kuskowski
    - Ages 7-10   Grades 2-5

- *Touch a Butterfly* by April Pulley  Sayre - Adult reading level
    - Part of the "Gardening with Kids" series

- *Design Your Own Butterfly Garden* by Susan Sales Harkins
    - Ages 7-10    Grades 2-5

www.ingramcontent.com/pod-product-compliance
Lightning Source LLC
Chambersburg PA
CBHW081639040426
42449CB00014B/3383